For my Dad, who taught me all about
hard work and dedication.—Kate

GROSSET & DUNLAP
Published by the Penguin Group
Penguin Group (USA) Inc., 375 Hudson Street, New York, New York 10014, USA
Penguin Group (Canada), 90 Eglinton Avenue East, Suite 700, Toronto, Ontario M4P 2Y3, Canada
(a division of Pearson Penguin Canada Inc.)
Penguin Books Ltd., 80 Strand, London WC2R 0RL, England
Penguin Group Ireland, 25 St. Stephen's Green, Dublin 2, Ireland
(a division of Penguin Books Ltd.)
Penguin Group (Australia), 250 Camberwell Road, Camberwell, Victoria 3124, Australia
(a division of Pearson Australia Group Pty. Ltd.)
Penguin Books India Pvt. Ltd., 11 Community Centre, Panchsheel Park, New Delhi—110 017, India
Penguin Group (NZ), 67 Apollo Drive, Rosedale, North Shore 0632, New Zealand
(a division of Pearson New Zealand Ltd.)
Penguin Books (South Africa) (Pty.) Ltd., 24 Sturdee Avenue,
Rosebank, Johannesburg 2196, South Africa

Penguin Books Ltd., Registered Offices:
80 Strand, London WC2R 0RL, England

Photo credits: cover: © Jeff Roberson/AP Images; copyright page: © Robert E. Klein/Getty Images;
title page: © Doug Mills/AP Images; page 5: © Doug Mills/Getty Images; page 9: © Rick Stewart/AP
Images; page 10: © Tom Pidgeon/Getty Images; page 16: © Rob Carr/AP Images; page 18: © Hans
Deryk/AP Images; page 19: © Michael Dwyer/AP Images; page 21: © Elise Amendola/AP Images;
page 23: © David J. Phillip/AP Images; page 24: © Peter Cosgrove/AP Images; page 26: © Elise
Amendola/AP Images; page 27: © Stephan Savoia/AP Images; page 29: © Brett Coomer/AP Images;
page 30: © Victoria Arocho/AP Images; page 32: © Stephan Savoia/AP Images; page 34: © Robert
E. Klein/AP Images; page 37: © Timothy A. Clary/Getty Images; page 38: © Thos Robinson/Getty
Images; page 40: © Tom Walck/PR Photos; page 41: © Henny Ray Abrams/AP Images; page 43: ©
Winslow Townson/AP Images; page 45: © Michael Dwyer/AP Images; page 47: © Any Lyons/ AP
Images.

Library of Congress Control Number: 2008005232

ISBN 978-0-448-44983-8   10 9 8 7 6 5 4 3 2 1

TOM BRADY
★ CHAMPION TEAMMATE ★

By Kate Ritchey

with photographs

Grosset & Dunlap

SIMPLY SUPER

The score was 17–17. The New England Patriots were on their own 17-yard line, and there was only 1:21 left to play in the game. The noise in the stadium was deafening. And the football was in the hands of Tom Brady.

Calmly, Brady called the plays. He threw the ball five yards. Eight yards. Eleven yards. Twenty-three yards. Six yards. With seven seconds left in the game, Brady handed the ball over to his kicker, who kicked a perfect field goal. Now there was no reason to play into overtime: The Patriots had won!

The last-second win would have been exciting in any game, but this was Super Bowl XXXVI! The Patriots had just won their first Super Bowl title! And 24-year-

old quarterback Tom Brady had helped
to get them there.

Brady celebrates his first Super Bowl championship on February 3, 2002.

CALIFORNIA COOL

Thomas Edward Brady Jr. was born on August 3, 1977. He is the youngest child of Galynn and Thomas Sr. and has three sisters, Maureen, Julie, and Nancy. Tom grew up in San Mateo, California.

Sports were always important in Tom's life. He went to a high school where several star athletes had gone, including Lynn Swann and Barry Bonds. His favorite football team, the San Francisco 49ers, became a football superpower while Tom was growing up. Their quarterback, Joe Montana, was Tom's idol.

Tom liked competing in anything from sports to video games. He wasn't a very good loser, though. But instead of just being angry about losing, he tried to improve so that he could win next time.

Tom loved football, but his parents wouldn't let him play until his freshman year of high school. They were afraid he would get hurt. Instead, he played baseball, soccer, and basketball. Baseball was his favorite sport next to football, and he played from Little League through high school. He was a catcher, and he was really good! He was so good in high school that in 1995 he was drafted by the Montreal Expos. But Major League Baseball wasn't Tom's dream.

When he began playing football for the Padres at Junípero Serra High School, Tom was only a backup quarterback. But in Tom's sophomore year, the junior varsity starting quarterback got hurt and he had a chance to be the starter. Tom finished his junior and senior years as the school's varsity starting quarterback.

Tom was a good player, but he wasn't a superstar yet. But what did stand out was his drive to succeed. He was constantly pushing himself. When he didn't think the squad's training routine was enough of a challenge, he even developed his own regimen. The team eventually adopted his jump-rope workout into their own routine!

By the time he finished high school, Tom had won several sports awards. He had thrown for just over 3,700 yards, and had passed for thirty-one touchdowns. Tom was named MVP at a football camp at the University of California. But Tom needed to work harder if he wanted to play football in college. Tom's dad sent highlight videos to the college coaches. When the offers finally came in, Tom chose to leave California. He was headed to the University of Michigan and the Big Ten.

IT'S GREAT TO BE A MICHIGAN WOLVERINE!

When Tom joined the Wolverines at the University of Michigan in 1995, he was redshirted at first. That meant he could practice with the team, but he

Brady sets up a play as a Michigan Wolverine in 1998.

couldn't play in games. In his second year, he was the third-string quarterback. He only got off the bench twice that year. But he worked hard off the field to make sure he would be ready when his chance came.

During his sophomore year, Tom played backup to the team's starting quarterback, Brian Griese. He got to play only four times.

Brady hangs his head in frustration.

Tom was frustrated by the lack of playing time. He knew he was good, and he wanted a chance to show it. He even thought about switching schools. But he stayed at Michigan and waited until Griese graduated for his chance to play. In his junior year he became the team's starting quarterback.

Tom played well that year, and the Wolverines ended with a 10-3 record. Tom completed 61.1 percent of his passes and had fifteen touchdowns. Things looked good for the young quarterback—but during his senior year, he faced another challenge.

Drew Henson, a sophomore, was going to split playing time with the senior quarterback. Tom would start the game, and then Henson would play the second quarter. Then at halftime, the coaches would decide who would finish the game. It was an unusual situation that must have been very frustrating for competitive Tom.

During the first five games of the season, the coaches chose to let Tom start after halftime. But in a game against Michigan State, Henson started the second half. The Wolverines lost the game 34–31. The two quarterbacks split playing time only once more, in another loss. After only seven games, Tom was back to being Michigan's full-time quarterback. The team won the next five games and ended the season 10-2.

In the final game of his college career, Tom played in the Orange Bowl against the University of Alabama. It was a great game for the quarterback, who completed 34 of 46 passes, threw for 369 yards, and had four touchdown passes. The

Wolverines won the game 35–34.

When Tom was finished with college, he wanted to play professional football. So he entered the NFL Draft. Professional teams use the draft to pick new players.

Unfortunately, the playing time Tom had split with Henson did not look good to NFL scouts. They thought that if he were a great player, he wouldn't have had to share the field. His scouting reports weren't very flattering, either. One scout wrote, "Poor build. Very skinny and narrow . . . Looks a little frail and lacks great physical stature and strength . . ." But Tom felt sure that an NFL team would recognize his talent and draft him.

As he sat watching the NFL Draft with his family, Tom got more and more nervous. The rounds kept going by, and his name hadn't been called. He was really hoping to be drafted by the 49ers, his favorite team. By the sixth round, he started to wonder: Would any of the teams pick him?

Finally, near the end of the sixth round of the 2000 NFL Draft, Tom Brady was selected. He was the 199th overall draft pick (out of 254 picks), and he was headed for the New England Patriots.

BRADY'S BIG CHANCE

During Brady's first year in the NFL, he was the backup fourth-string quarterback. He played only once, against the Detroit Lions. Mostly he played on the practice team.

The owner of the Patriots, Robert Kraft, liked Brady's confidence right away. The first time they met, Kraft said to him, "You're Tom Brady, our sixth-round pick out of Michigan." Brady answered, "And I'm the best decision this organization ever made." He was sure of himself without being conceited, and the owner knew he was something special.

Still, Brady knew he had to improve to play with the regular team. One day he peeked inside quarterback coach Dick Rehbein's evaluation notebook and saw a

Brady gets a first down against the Baltimore Ravens.

note about himself. It said that he was too slow, that he needed to be quicker. If he wanted to play, Brady had to show the coaches what he was capable of achieving.

And so even though he knew he probably wouldn't play soon, Brady prepared like he would. He gained fifteen pounds of muscle and worked on increasing his speed. He watched hours of practices and games on tape. He memorized the team's playbook. He watched the veteran players and learned from them. He wanted to be ready for any chance that came his way.

Little did Brady know that his big chance would come in the second game of the 2001 season. The Patriots were losing when the team's star quarterback, Drew Bledsoe, was tackled hard by New York Jets linebacker Mo Lewis. The

beloved quarterback was hurt so badly
that he was taken out of the game. He
was replaced by Brady.

With 2:16 left in the fourth quarter,
Brady ran onto the field. He moved the
Patriots 45 yards in twelve plays, but it
wasn't enough to win.

The next game, against the
Indianapolis Colts, was Brady's very first
as an NFL starting quarterback. He led
the team to a 44–13 win over their

division
rivals.
Brady con-
tinued to
play while
Bledsoe
recovered,
winning
five games

Brady celebrates after throwing a touchdown pass.

and losing only three.

In mid-November, Bledsoe was cleared to play by the medical team. He was ready to take back his position. But coach Belichick decided that Brady should continue as the team's starting quarterback.

Patriots fans were divided over the decision. Many wanted Bledsoe back, but others thought that Brady showed promise. He wasn't a star yet, but he definitely was helping the team win games. He set his first NFL record in his sixth game as a starter: He threw 162 passes before his first career interception. And with a win over the Buffalo Bills on November 11, the Patriots had a winning record (5-4) for the first time in almost two years.

In the first game after he had been announced as the full-time starting quarterback, Brady showed New England fans that Belichick had made the right decision. He threw 258 yards and four touchdowns in the win against the New Orleans Saints. In fact, Brady and the Patriots won the last six games in their regular season. The last-place AFC East team from 2000 was now the first-place team in 2001!

In the first game of the postseason, the Patriots played the Oakland Raiders in the middle of a blizzard. The Patriots were down by three points in the fourth quarter when Brady was hit from behind, the football knocked away from him. The Raiders recovered the ball and took away New England's chances of winning with it. But when officials reviewed the play, they reversed their decision. The Patriots kept the ball and tied the game with a field goal by kicker Adam Vinatieri, sending

Brady loses the ball after being tackled from behind by a Raiders defenseman.

the game into overtime. The ace kicker scored another field goal in overtime to win the game.

Next, the Patriots traveled to Pittsburgh, where they played the Steelers for the conference title. When Brady sprained his ankle on a hit in the second quarter, Bledsoe came into the game and led the team to its first AFC title since 1997. It was his last game as a Patriot.

On February 3, 2002, Tom Brady and the Patriots met the St. Louis Rams in the New Orleans Superdome for Super Bowl XXXVI. The Patriots were expected to lose to the Rams, who had the best regular-season record in the NFL (14-2).

When it was time for the teams to take the field, the Rams entered one at a time as each player's name was announced. But the Patriots ran out together as a team.

The Patriots reach for the Vince Lombardi Trophy after winning the Super Bowl.

They were a jumping, bouncing mass of red, white, and blue uniforms. After a great three quarters, the Rams scored fourteen points in the fourth quarter to tie the Patriots. It was 17–17 with 1:21 left to play, and Tom Brady had the ball.

Keeping a cool head under presure, Brady led his team to victory. Adam Vinatieri once again came onto the field to score the game-winning field goal. And suddenly, the Patriots were the champions.

Red, white, and blue confetti fell everywhere. Brady was voted the MVP of Super Bowl XXXVI. At the time, he was the youngest quarterback to win a Super Bowl.

After flying to Disney World as the MVP, Brady returned to Boston for a Patriots victory parade. An estimated 1.25 million people showed up to celebrate the team in City Hall Plaza. Then he went on to play in the Pro Bowl in Hawaii before his spectacular season came to a close. Tom Brady, last year's fourth-string quarterback, was finally on top.

RETURN TO THE SUPER BOWL

The Patriots' 2002 season did not turn out anything like the 2001 season. The team won its first three games, but ended the season with a 9-7 record.

Brady had some amazing moments in 2002, but it wasn't a great season for him. He threw a career-high 410 yards in a game against the Kansas City Chiefs. He had twenty-eight touchdown passes that year, the most in the league. But he also had fourteen interceptions. Other teams found a way to stop him. In the last month of the season, he averaged only 167.8 yards per game. To make it worse, he injured his right shoulder (his throwing shoulder) in the season's final game against the Dolphins. He did manage a come-from-behind win in that final game, reminding fans of his last-minute wins from 2001. But the Patriots did not make it to the playoffs. Brady spent the off-season preparing to make 2003 great.

The 2003 season began with a jolt. In the very first game, the Patriots played the Buffalo Bills. Brady tied his career-high four interceptions. The Patriots lost the game 31–0.

After the first loss, things began to

Brady struggles in a game against the Denver Broncos.

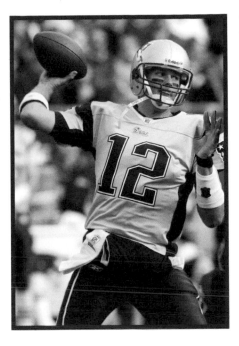

look up. People started to know Brady as the quarterback who didn't make dumb mistakes, who had all the right moves.

In the very last game of the regular season, the Patriots made up for their first game disaster against Buffalo. They won the game 31–0. Brady had four touchdown passes before halftime.

The divisional playoff game with the Titans was freezing. It was 4°F with a windchill of -10. But the Patriots weren't stopped. They won 17–14 and headed into the AFC Championship against the Colts.

The Patriots defense shone in the conference championship matchup, intercepting four of Colts quarterback Peyton Manning's throws. New England won the game 24–14, and for the second time, Brady and the Patriots were headed to the Super Bowl.

On February 1, 2004, the Patriots met the Carolina Panthers at Houston's Reliant Stadium for Super Bowl XXXVIII. With less than two minutes left in the game, the teams were tied 29–29. But Brady got the football at the Patriots' 40-yard line with 1:08 left to play. Brady marched his team down the field to put kicker Vinatieri in position to kick a field goal. He kicked it from the Panthers' 23-yard line, and again the Patriots won the Super Bowl by a field goal in the final seconds of the game.

And as the red, white, and blue confetti fell, Tom Brady won the Super Bowl MVP award for the second time in three years. He had thrown for 354 yards, tossed three touchdowns, and completed 32 of his 48 passes! This was a record for the most completions ever

Adam Vinatieri kicks the winning field goal in the 2004 Super Bowl.

thrown in a Super Bowl. All that was left for Brady's season was to head to Disney World and then back to Boston for the celebration parade—again.

Brady waves to fans as he rides along the Super Bowl parade route in Boston.

A PATRIOTS DYNASTY

Before the 2004 season started,
Brady's injured shoulder needed surgery.
He had minor surgery and was ready to
play when the season began.

Brady and the Patriots had ended
their last season with fifteen straight wins.
They kept winning until game seven
of 2004, when the Pittsburgh Steelers
beat them 34–20. The twenty-one-game
winning streak, from October 5, 2003,
through October 31, 2004, was the
longest in NFL history.

The loss was hard for Brady, but
he and the Patriots bounced back. The
Patriots ended their season 14-2, winning
their division. When they met the Colts
and NFL MVP Peyton Manning for the
divisional playoff, they didn't allow the

Colts a single touchdown.

The AFC Championship game was a rematch with the Steelers. But this time, New England was ready. In the end, the Patriots were the AFC champions for the second year in a row, with a score of 41–27.

On February 6, 2005, Tom Brady and the Patriots played the Philadelphia Eagles in Super Bowl XXXIX. In the fourth quarter, the Patriots were ahead,

Brady leads his team one step closer to winning Super Bowl XXXIX.

24–21. With under a minute to play, the Eagles held the football.

Philadelphia began their final drive with forty-six seconds to go. Eagles quarterback Donovan McNabb tried to move his team down the field, but Patriots defensive back Rodney Harrison intercepted McNabb's toss. For the third time in four years, the New England Patriots were Super Bowl champions.

This win gave Brady a 9-0 postseason record and his team a 32-4 record over two years. Brady was also voted into the Pro Bowl for the second time.

With their third Super Bowl win, people began to call the Patriots a dynasty, like the Cowboys, the 49ers, the Steelers, and the Packers were years ago. The team had dominated the NFL, and they planned to keep on going.

INJURIES AND LOSSES

Unfortunately, the next two seasons were not filled with the championships of Brady's early years as a Patriot. Defensive coordinator Romeo Crennel and offensive coordinator Charlie Weis, Brady's mentor, both left the team at the end of the 2004 season. Tedy Bruschi, a longtime New England inside linebacker, had a stroke soon after the 2004 season. He recovered quickly, returning to play in the Patriots' sixth game of the 2005 season, but his absence

Brady takes a seat on the sidelines.

was felt while he was out. And at least six major players changed teams during the off-season.

Brady had another good season in 2005. He completed 334 of 530 throws for 4,110 yards, the most total yards in his career to that point and the most in the NFL that year. He also won the *Sports Illustrated* Sportsman of the Year award. Brady was excited to get the award, which only five other professional football players had received.

The Patriots went 10-6 in the regular season, winning their division for the third year in a row. They won their first play-off game against the Jacksonville Jaguars, 28–3. With that game Brady set an NFL record, improving to ten consecutive wins in the postseason. But on January 14, 2006, the Patriots lost to the Denver

Broncos in the divisional championship. The Patriots' season, and Brady's postgame winning streak, were over.

The 2006 season was another heartbreaker. Before the season began, newly appointed defensive coordinator Eric Mangini left the team. More than five of the Patriots' major players left, too, including kicker Vinatieri, who helped win so many last-second games.

Brady kept up his great quarterbacking. His year wasn't as good as 2005, but he still led the team to a 12-4 record and a fourth consecutive AFC East title. The Patriots defeated both the New York Jets and the San Diego Chargers in the playoffs. Then they played the Colts in the AFC championship. New England was winning at halftime, 21–6, but Indianapolis came back to win, 38–34. In the final minute of the game, Brady was marching his team toward the end zone as he had so many times before. But this time one of his passes was intercepted, and the game was over.

Determined as always to improve himself, Brady spent the off-season preparing for 2007. He didn't know yet that it would be the best he'd ever had.

Brady talks to his teammates in a huddle.

A PUBLIC PRIVATE LIFE

Before Tom Brady's roller-coaster 2001 season, people didn't believe him when he said he played for the Patriots. He was sent to the back of lines at clubs, and girls wouldn't talk to him. He and his friends could go out for dinner and no one paid any attention.

But since his first year as a starter catapulted him

to fame, Tom has been on the covers of magazines, in advertisments, and in television interviews. He can no longer go out without being mobbed by people wanting autographs and pictures.

He's very good at handling his fame on the playing field. Tom is well aware that he didn't achieve success alone, and he's quick to praise his teammates, coaches, and family. If a player doesn't catch one of his passes, he's the first to say it was a bad throw. He's not a show-off or a boaster, and his teammates really like him.

Tom knows that in football the team is more important than the individual, and he enjoys being part of it. "[T]he most meaningful accomplishments are always the ones I have celebrated with my teammates," he said. When he wins awards or is praised by the media, he always credits his team. He is truly a champion teammate.

Off the field, Tom rarely does

television interviews (other than his weekly press conferences). He doesn't do many endorsement deals, and keeps his personal life as personal as he can.

Of course, that's never easy when the world wants to know all about you! The media follow Tom and report on everything he does. Sightings of the New England player in a Yankees cap made front-page news in Boston, and gossip

columns love to write about his romantic life. Tom dated actress Bridget Moynahan for three years, and the couple had a son together. John Edward Thomas

Moynahan was born on August 22, 2007, just before his father's historic Patriots season.

Tom is very close to his family (who always call him Tommy, never Tom). One of his sisters lives near him in Boston, and the rest of the family frequently flies across the country to watch him play. When they can't be there, they gather to watch the game together on TV. "It's unbelievable what he's accomplished," said his sister Maureen during Tom's 2007 season. And she was right.

Brady and his parents after winning Sports Illustrated *Sportsman of the Year.*

A SEASON TO REMEMBER

The 2007 season was something special for Brady and the New England Patriots. They were undefeated in the regular season, and broke many records along the way. They broke the NFL regular-season records for touchdowns (75), total points (589), and consecutive wins (19). They outscored their opponents by 315 points during the regular season, setting another record. They were also the first NFL team ever to go 16-0 during their regular season.

Brady led his team to many outstanding victories in 2007. Some of the games were close, but many of them had incredible scores, like 52–7 and 56–10. One of Brady's best games of the season was against the Miami Dolphins on October

Brady looks downfield for a receiver.

21. He completed 21 of 25 passes for 354 yards and six touchdown passes. He ended the game with a perfect quarterback rating of 158.3.

During the regular season, Brady broke many individual records. He had the most passing yards of any Patriots quarterback in team history. He also threw at least three touchdowns in ten straight games to set an NFL record. In the last game of the regular season, Brady broke the record for most touchdown passes in a season (50). At the end of his amazing regular season, Brady was awarded football's highest individual honor: the NFL Most Valuable Player award.

On January 12, 2008, the Patriots played the Jacksonville Jaguars in the divisional playoff. Brady played a great game. Brady set even more records on the

way to this win. He completed his first
sixteen pass attempts, breaking an NFL
postseason record. He also broke the
record for the highest pass completion
percentage with 26 of 28 attempts. Finally,
he set the playoff record for highest
quarterback rating with a 141.4 rating.

After beating the San Diego Chargers
to become the AFC champions, Brady and
the Patriots met the New York Giants in
Super Bowl XLII. It was Brady's fourth

The Patriots line up against the New York Giants.

Super Bowl in seven years, but unfortunately it didn't end like his first three. After an exciting fourth quarter, the Giants scored a touchdown with thirty-nine seconds left to play. Brady and his team weren't able to come back in the time remaining, and the Patriots lost the game 17–14.

Despite the disappointing end to the season, 2007 was Tom Brady's best year yet. And with his determination to better himself, who knows what else he is capable of. He has only been playing in the NFL for eight years, and he has already had a remarkable career. What's next for Brady? With Brady's talent, positive attitude, and hard work, the sky is the limit.

TOM BRADY'S RECORD BOOK

★ First quarterback to win three Super Bowls before his 28th birthday

★ Most consecutive playoff wins (10)

★ Most pass completions in any Super Bowl (32 in Super Bowl XXXVIII)

★ Best record in regular season and playoff games in the Super Bowl era of the NFL (100-27)

★ Most overtime wins without a defeat (7-0)

TOM BRADY'S 2007 RECORDS

★ Most touchdown passes in a season (50)

★ Most passing yards in a season of any Patriots quarterback (4,806)

★ Highest completion percentage in a game (with a minimum of 20 passes thrown) (92.9 percent)

★ Playoff record for quarterback rating in a game (141.4)

★ Straight games with at least three touchdowns (10)

★ Postseason record for consecutive completed passes (16)

★ Fewest games needed by a starting quarterback to reach 100 wins (126 games)

★ Games in a regular season with at least three touchdown passes (12)